CW01673486

Roni la Rana

ROH-nee lah RAH-nah

Roni the frog

Written by Nicola Maguire
Illustrated by Ivy Trazsi

SilverWood

Nicola – for my inspiring niece Arianne, who loves languages
Ivy – for my best friend Tao, who is both kind and curious

Published in 2021 by SilverWood Books

SilverWood Books Ltd
14 Small Street, Bristol, BS1 1DE, United Kingdom
www.silverwoodbooks.co.uk

ISBN 978-1-80042-056-4 (paperback)
ISBN 978-1-80042-172-1 (ebook)

British Library Cataloguing in Publication Data
A CIP catalogue record for this book is available from the British Library

Audio by Uxía Iglesias Fuertes
Typesetting by SilverWood Books

Scan for the audio recording of *Roni la Rana*

Roni lives in the jungle with her family and friends. She is a Splendid Leaf Frog which is native to South America. She has a yellow stripe on her chin which makes her look rather distinguished; one of the more splendid, Splendid Leaf Frogs.

The pronunciation in this book is based on European Spanish.

¡Hola a todo el mundo!

OH-lah ah TOH-doh ehl MOON-doh!

Hello everyone!

In order to gain the most from this book:

- First of all, read the phonics aloud slowly as you build confidence in your pronunciation, focusing on which part of the word to emphasise (in capital letters).
- Do not be afraid of sounding silly! You will be using sounds you are not used to, and some of them may not be quite what you expect. The more you read them, the more familiar they will become and your child will be in awe!
- You can also listen to the audio provided at the front of the book whilst following along with the written Spanish to support your pronunciation.
- By reading Spanish regularly to your child, they will get more used to Spanish language sounds which studies show will build new connections in their magnificent brains and will not interfere with their first language acquisition.
- As with any child's story time, there are no rules, so you can choose to skip to certain sections you'd like to practise. E.g. How Roni greets her friends or numbers.
- You could also read the story in English and talk through the illustrations to help you remember the meaning of the words.
- Read it to your child at any time of day; whilst they're playing, eating or at bedtime, alongside their other favourite books.

For free resources and more information on the benefits of language learning, go to www.ronifonix.com

¡Hola! Me llamo Roni.

OH-lah! Meh YAH-moh ROH-nee.

Hello! I'm called Roni.

Soy una rana espléndida.

Soy OO-nah RAH-nah ehs-PLEHN-dee-dah.

I'm a splendid leaf frog.

¿Cómo estás?

KOH-moh ehs-TAHS?

How are you?

Vivo en una casa de árbol

BEE-boh ehn OO-nah KAH-sah deh AHR-bohl

I live in a treehouse

en la selva.

ehn lah SEHL-bah.

in the jungle.

Y tengo una barbilla amarilla...

Ee TEHN-goh OO-nah bahr-BEE-yah ah-mah-REE-yah...

And I have a yellow chin...

como mi madre.

KOH-moh mee MAH-dreh.

like my Mum.

Me encanta saltar

Meh ehn-KAHN-tah sahl-TAHR

I love jumping

y bailar salsa.

ee bah-ee-LAHR SAHL-sah.

and dancing salsa.

Pero sobre todo,

PEH-roh SOH-breh TOH-doh,

But especially,

me encantan los panqueques.
meh ehn-KAHN-tahn lohs pahn-KEH-kehs.
I love pancakes.

¡Y las aventuras!
Ee lahs ah-behn-TOO-rahs!
And adventures!

Estoy lista para una aventura.
Ehs-TOY LEES-tah PAH-rah OO-nah ah-behn-TOO-rah.
I'm ready for an adventure.

¿Y tú?
Ee too?
And you?

¿Sí?
See?
Yes?

Bueno, ¡vamos!
BWEH-noh, BAH-mohs!
Right, let's go!

Pero, ¿dónde estás?
PEH-roh, DOHN-deh ehs-TAHS?
But, where are you?

No te veo.
Noh teh BEH-oh.
I don't see you.

¿Estás...
Ehs-TAHS...
Are you...

en la montaña?
ehn lah mohn-TAH-nyah?
in the mountains?

Veo a mi amigo Ron, el cóndor.
BEH-oh ah mee ah-MEE-goh Rohn, ehl KOHN-dohr.
I see my friend Ron, the condor.

¡Buenos días, Ron!
BWEH-nohs DEE-ahs, Rohn!
Good morning, Ron!

¡Buenos días, Roni!
BWEH-nohs DEE-ahs, ROH-nee!
Good morning, Roni!

¿Qué tal?
Keh tahl?
How are you?

¡Genial!
Heh-NYAHL!
Great!

¡Mírame!
MEE-rah-meh!
Look at me!

¡Te veo!
Teh BEH-oh!
I see you!

¡Pero no te veo a ti!
PEH-roh noh teh BEH-oh ah tee!
But I don't see you!

¿Dónde estás?
DOHN-deh ehs-TAHS?
Where are you?

¿Estás...
Ehs-TAHS...
Are you...

...en el lago?
...ehn ehl LAH-goh?
...at the lake?

Veo a mi amiga Rosa, la mariposa.
BEH-oh ah mee ah-MEE-gah ROH-sah, lah mah-ree-POH-sah.
I see my friend Rosa, the butterfly.

¡Buenas tardes, Rosa!
BWEH-nahs TAHR-dehs, ROH-sah!
Good afternoon, Rosa!

¡Buenas tardes, Roni!
BWEH-nahs TAHR-dehs, ROH-nee!
Good afternoon, Roni!

¡Cómo estás?

KOH-moh ehs-TAHS?

How are you?

Bien,

Byehn,

Good,

¡Mírame!

MEE-rah-meh!

Watch me!

¡Te veo!

Teh BEH-oh!

I see you!

¿Cuántos flamencos hay?

KWAHN-tohs flah-MEHN-kohs ah-ee?

How many flamingos are there?

Uno

OO-noh

One

dos

dohs

two

tres

trehs

three

cuatro
KWAH-troh
four

cinco
THEEN-koh
five

¡seis!
seh-ees!
six!

Pero, ¿dónde ESTÁS TÚ?
PEH-roh, DOHN-deh ehs-TAHS too?
But, where ARE YOU?

¿Estás...
Ehs-TAHS...
Are you...

en la selva?
ehn lah SEHL-bah?
in the jungle?

¿Cuántos monos hay?
KWAHN-tohs MOH-nohs ah-ee?
How many monkeys are there?

Uno, dos, tres
OO-noh, dohs, trehs
one, two, three

cuatro, cinco, seis
KWAH-troh, THEEN-koh, seh-ees
four, five, six

¡siete!
SYEH-teh!
seven!

Veo a mi amigo Paco, el mono bolsillo.

BEH-oh ah mee ah-MEE-goh PAH-koh, ehl MOH-noh bohl-SEE-yoh.

I see my friend Paco, the pocket monkey.

¡Hola, Roni!

OH-lah, ROH-nee!

Hi, Roni!

¡Hola, Paco!

OH-lah, PAH-koh!

Hi, Paco!

Pero no te veo.

PEH-roh noh teh BEH-oh.

But I don't see you.

¿Dónde estás?

DOHN-deh Ehs-TAHS?

Where are you?

¿Estás...

Ehs-TAHS..

Are you...

en la costa?

ehn lah KOHS-tah?

on the coast?

Hay muchos peces

Ah-ee MOO-chos PEH-thehs.

There are lots of fish.

¿Cuántos peces hay?

KWAHN-tohs PEH-thehs ah-ee?

How many fish are there?

Uno

OO-noh

One

dos

dohs

two

tres

trehs

three

cuatro
KWAH-troh
four

cinco
THEEN-koh
five

seis
seh-ees
six

siete
SYEH-teh
seven

¡ocho!
OH-choh!
eight!

Veo a mi amigo Octavio, el pulpo.

BEH-oh ah mee ah-MEE-goh ohk-TAH-byoh, ehl POOL-poh.

I see my friend Octavio, the octopus.

¡Hola, Octavio!

OH-lah, ohk-TAH-byoh!

Hello, Octavio!

¡Hola! ¿Qué tal, Roni?

OH-lah! Keh tahl, ROH-nee?

Hi! How are you, Roni?

Muy bien. ¿Y tú?

Mwee byehn. Ee too?

Very good. And you?

¡Estupendo!

Ehs-too-PEHN-doh!

Wonderful!

¡Mírame!
MEE-rah-meh!
Look at me!

¡No te veo!
Noh teh BEH-oh!
I don't see you!

Y tú, ¿dónde estás?
Ee too? DOHN-deh ehs-TAHS?
And you? Where are you?

¿Estás...
Ehs-TAHS...
Are you...

en la playa?
ehn lah PLAH-yah?
on the beach?

¿Cuántas estrellas de mar hay?
KWAHN-tahs ehs-TREH-yas deh mahr ah-ee?
How many starfish are there?

Una
OO-nah
One

dos
dohs
two

tres
trehs
three

cuatro
KWAH-troh
four
cinco
THEEN-koh
five
seis
seh-ees
six
siete
SYEH-teh
seven
ocho
OH-choh
eight
¡nueve!
NWEH-beh!
nine!

Veo a mi mejor amiga,
BEH-oh ah mee meh-HOHR ah-MEE-gah,
I see my best friend,

Arruga, la tortuga.
Ah-RROO-gah, lah tohr-TOO-gah.
Wrinkle, the tortoise.

¡Hola, Arruga!
OH-lah, ah-RROO-gah!
Hello, Wrinkle!

¿Cómo estás?
KOH-moh ehs-TAHS?
How are you?

¡Fenomenal!
Feh-noh-meh-NAHL!
Amazing!

¡Mírame!
MEE-rah-meh!
Look at me!

¡Jajaja! ¡No te veo!
Hahaha! Noh teh BEH-oh!
Hahaha! I don't see you!

Bueno, tengo que irme a casa.
BWEH-noh, TEHN-goh keh EER-meh ah KAH-sah.
Right, I have to go home.

¿Dónde ESTÁS?
DOHN-deh ehs-TAHS?
Where ARE YOU?

¡Ahí estás!

Ah-EE ehs-TAHS!

There you are!

¿Cuántas ranas hay en mi familia?

KWAHN-tahs RAH-nas ah-ee ehn mee fah-MEE-lyah?

How many frogs are there in my family?

Una
OO-nah
One

dos
dohs
two

tres
trehs
three

cuatro
KWAH-troh
Four

cinco
THEEN-koh
five

seis
seh-ees
six

siete
SYEH-teh
seven

ocho
OH-choh
eight

nueve
NWEH-beh
nine

y yo...¡diez!
ee yoh...dyeth!
and me...ten!

Ay, tengo hambre.
Ah-ee, TEHN-goh AHM-breh.
Phew, I'm hungry.

Quiero comer...
KYEH-roh koh-MEHR...
I want to eat...

¡Panqueques!
Pahn-KEH-kehs!
Pancakes!

¡Ñam ñam!
Nyam nyam!
Yum yum!

Once you learn the main pronunciation rules in Spanish, you will be easily understood by Spanish speakers everywhere.

The key vowel sounds which are found throughout this book are:

a pronounced ah (rana, etc.) and sounds like the ‘a’ in cat.

e pronounced eh (me, tres, etc.) and sounds like the ‘e’ in egg.

i pronounced ee (cinco, etc.) and sounds like the ‘i’ in Bolivia (and Bristol!)

o pronounced oh (Cómo, etc.) and sounds like the ‘o’ in octopus.

u pronounced oo (uno, etc.) and sounds like the ‘oo’ in igloo.

Did you spot any other pronunciation rules?

llamo (YAH-moh) – ‘ll’ sounds like a ‘y’.

ñam ñam (nyam nyam) – ‘ñ’ sounds like ‘gn’ in lasagne.

aventuras (ah-behn-TOOR-ahs) – ‘v’ sounds like a ‘b’.

qué (keh) – ‘qu’ sounds like a ‘k’.

arruga (ah-RROO-gah) – ‘rr’ – try to roll your tongue!

Go to www.ronifonix.com for key vocabulary and grammar from this book and lots more free resources!

Lightning Source UK Ltd.
Milton Keynes UK
UKHW050354290921
391350UK00002B/27